GLOBAL SUPPLY CHAIN MANAGEMENT AND THE IMPACT OF TECHNOLOGY: A STUDY

DR. CHANTELL BEATY

Dr. Beaty is a Doctor of Business Administration (DBA) – with special reference to International Business and Marketing at Walden University, Minneapolis, Minnesota, United States. A certified researcher and Bottom of the Pyramid (BOP) economic specialist with extensive research and study in BOP markets. Doctoral research study: Business Leaders Marketing to Bottom of the Pyramid Consumers of Nigeria. Dr. Beaty has over 25 years in business administration. Dr. Beaty's careers include an extensive profile of experience with the United States Federal Government, GSA; Department of Homeland Security, FEMA (Unsung Heroes Award); and Department of Defense, United States Air Force, civilian duty. Dr. Beaty's background in education extends from teaching at the local college to teaching as a certified math teacher in a range of grades from elementary to high school, special education to gifted and talented, and now managing her own start up University for business leaders of the world. Dr. Beaty's business ownership background covers a broad range of business knowledge and ownership from sales director to international researcher and consultant. Dr. Beaty is an International Gold Key Scholar, and holds a Bachelor's of Science (BS) and Masters of Business Administration (MBA) from Texas Wesleyan University.

C.R. Beaty & Associates

Global Supply Chain Management and the Impact of Technology: A Study Analysis

Dr. Chantell Beaty

Abstract

Supply chains, supply chain management, and global supply chain management are terms that researchers use to create and manage products domestically and globally. There are various trends and innovations to supply chain management. Researchers reveal gaps in the literature and the need for continued research. Global supply chain management and technology is a trending aspect of supply chain management and leads to the enhancement of organization based on further research and studies. The researcher presents a background, analysis of the field and future contribution to supply chain management in terms of global supply chain management and technology.

Table of Contents

Global Supply Chain and the Impact of Technology 3

Supply Chain Management and Supply Chain 3

Global Supply Chain Management 4

Analysis of the Field 5
    Innovation and Trends 5
    Examples of Theories and Frameworks Used in Supply Chain Management 6
    Gaps in Literature 8

Global Supply Chain Management and Technology 9
    Design and Methodology 10
    Research Findings 10

Future Directions 11

Conclusion 12

Appendix A: An Example of a Global Supply Chain and Design 13

Appendix B: Annotated Bibliographies for Further Research 17

References 24

Global Supply Chain and the Impact of Technology

Technavio is a leading technology research and advisory firm with global coverage. Their analyst forecast that the global supply chain management (GSCM) market would grow at a compound annual growth rate (CAGR) of 10.73 percent over the period 2013-2018 (PR Newswire, 2014). This helps to substantiate a reason for further research into the impact of technology on GSCM. Therefore, I will present an analysis of research on GSCM and technology and future directions based on my research findings.

Supply Chain Management and Supply Chain

A working definition of supply chain management (SCM) including the integration of supply chains is the co-ordination and management of the upstream and downstream product, service, financial, and information flows of the core business processes between a focal company and its key suppliers and its key customers (Naslund & Hulthen, 2012). A supply chain is a network created amongst different companies producing, handling and/or distributing a specific product (Investopedia, 2015). This network encompasses the steps it takes to get a good or service from the supplier to the customer, and it includes every company that it encounters to create a particular product. (Investopedia, 2015). Supply chain management (SCM) is a critical process for many companies, and many companies strive to have the most optimized supply chain because it usually translates to lower costs for the company (Investopedia, 2015). SCM is not the same as logistics. In turn, logistics refers to the distribution process within the company whereas the supply chain includes multiple companies such as suppliers, manufacturers, and the retailers (Investopedia, 2015)

Global Supply Chain Management

Collaboration and overseas sourcing convey complexity and monitoring problems for smaller firms (Boyson, Corsi, Dresner, & Harrington, 2007). As a means to reduce costs, increase efficiencies, and boost profits, firms have integrated their operations with its suppliers and customers by managing its supply chain (Boyson, Corsi, Dresner, & Harrington, 2007).

In the age of globalization, suppliers and customers are in dispersed locations around the world, and achieving such integrated operations is not an easy task (Boyson, Corsi, Dresner, & Harrington, 2007). Failure of organizations to develop a supply-chain management program that fully accomplishes such integrated operations may result in poorly engineered products, product recalls, excess inventory costs, stockouts, and diminishing levels of customer satisfaction.

The GSCM market can be divided into five segments, namely, the warehouse management system, transportation management system, supply chain planning, procurement software, and manufacturing execution system segments (PR Newswire, 2014). Academic literature suggests that integration is a requirement and key characteristic for SCM and globalization is one reason for corporations to integrate their supply chain (Naslund & Hulthen, 2012).

The global crisis of 2008 multiplied the sources of supply chain uncertainty (Mamillo, 2015). Sources like unstable trade and capital flow, currency exchange risk, uncertainty about the environment regulations, and an increase of uncertainty regarding the decision of choosing suppliers as companies in developed countries became credible (Malik & Ruwadi, 2011). Supply chain uncertainty today is higher due to the global crisis, fast-changing technology, and the increasing vulnerability of supply chains (Mamillo, 2015). Companies now use different strategies to reduce uncertainty by building agile supply chains and increasing resilience. In addition, all these strategies require strong supply chain collaboration (Mamillo, 2015).

Analysis of the Field

An analysis of the state of the field of GSCM reveals that organizations in SCM are focusing on ways to enhance their supply chain strategies. They are forming strategic alliances with suppliers, collaborating in efforts of knowledge, meeting challenges of new product development (NPD), and extending research in supplier integration and NPD.

Innovation and Trends

An important issue in the field of GSCM is innovation and trends. Organizations in their practice of supply chain management (SCM) are forming strategic alliances with suppliers and requiring them to implement certifications (Wisner, 2000). In order to maximize the impact of supplier innovativeness, manufacturers should align with suppliers that have complementary learning styles (Azadegan, Dooley, Carter, & Carter, 2008).

Supply chain collaboration is one of the most important topics in the business of SCM, and not only because of its importance in supply chain management, but because it provides many benefits to the supply chain members as well (Mamillo, 2015). In addition, collaboration, as well as e-collaboration of supply chain partners, increases innovation by the pooling of their resources (Cassivi, Hadaya, Lefebvre, & Lefebvre, 2008); and also, positively impacts the operation of firms and their abilities to innovate (Soosay, Hyland, & Ferrer, 2008).

Moreover, since product development has increasingly become risky, expensive, and dependent on disparate knowledge, organizations are creating design models that incorporate their suppliers in order to meet these challenges (Handfield & Lawson, 2007). However, although research has expanded on supplier integration to the point of availability of contingencies, new product development (NPD) and supplier integration remain for extended research (Handfield, & Lawson, 2007).

Today's world of business was shaped by the trend of globalization while the expected life of a company got much shorter. The cutthroat competition in saturated markets, the growing scarcity of the resources, the quick exchange of information and the new technologies available worldwide mean that daily, a company has to face many challenges in order to survive. Moreover, the customers put pressure on companies by expecting from them cheap but high-quality products that are environment-friendly. This means that sustainability management in a company is no more a matter of choice, but an absolute must in order to keep the competitive advantage (Pivoda, 2014).

Examples of Theories and Frameworks Used in Supply Chain Management

Researchers use of customer relationship management (CRM) in generating growth and sustaining profitability in the tyre manufacturing industry of Zimbabwe led to the level of awareness of the relationship marketing concept within tyre manufacturing companies in Zimbabwe (Gotore, Mutanga, & Mugwati, 2014. Furthermore, researchers led to evaluate the level of adoption and implementation of relationship marketing by players within the tyre manufacturing industry and to find out the contribution to profitability and business growth of relationship marketing in the tyre manufacturing industry (Gotore, Mutanga, & Mugwati, 2014. Authors of the study recommend that tyre manufacturing companies broaden their view of customer relations and incorporate the use of information communication technology to help implement lifetime relationships with their clients and stimulate corporate growth (Gotore, Mutanga, & Mugwati, 2014. Authors of the study also recommended that the organizations undergo a culture reform and align all their employees in all departments, to the demands and needs of ideal and effective relationship (Gotore, Mutanga, & Mugwati, 2014).

The ability to answer questions about the safety and environmental effects of products we use is critical (Odenwald & Berg, 2014). However, without the right information, even seemingly easy questions are difficult to answer (Odenwald & Berg, 2014. We send spacecraft to Mars, but we know embarrassingly little about everyday products we use (Odenwald & Berg, 2014. Although we produce huge quantities of data every second, we frequently lack the relevant and actionable data points to respond to simple questions people have about what products are made of and how they are made (Odenwald & Berg, 2014). For the most part, today's information systems and reporting methods treat factors such as emissions, waste and employee protections as externalities (Odenwald & Berg, 2014). However, many factors, including economic uncertainty, population growth, and climate change and escalating demand for natural resources, are placing new pressures on companies to take a broader set of considerations into account when making decisions (Odenwald & Berg, 2014).

Researchers present a methodology for evaluating companies' degree of adherence to an SCM conceptual model (Simon, Di Serio, Pires, & Martins, 2015). The methodology is based on

Cooper, Lambert, and Pagh's original contribution and involves analysis of eleven referential axes established from key business processes, horizontal structures, and initiatives & practices (Simon, Di Serio, Pires, & Martins, 2015). The researchers analyze the applicability of the proposed model based on findings from interviews with experts - academics and practitioners - as well as from case studies of three focal firms and their supply chains (Simon, Di Serio, Pires, & Martins, 2015). In general, the methodology can be considered a diagnostic instrument that allows companies to evaluate their maturity regarding SCM practices (Simon, Di Serio, Pires, & Martins, 2015). From this diagnosis, firms can identify and implement activities to improve the degree of adherence to the reference model and achieve SCM benefits (Simon, Di Serio, Pires, & Martins, 2015). The methodology aims to contribute to SCM theory development. It is initial, but structured, reference for translating a theoretical approach into practical aspects (Simon, Di Serio, Pires, & Martins, 2015).

Gaps in Literature

New product development (NPD) and supplier integration remain for extended research (Handfield, & Lawson, 2007). Empirical studies on timing of integration with suppliers and level of integration with suppliers remain for exploration by researchers. Researchers found limited empirical research discussing SCM integration beyond the dyadic level, and there is a lack of empirical evidence supporting the claimed benefits of supply-chain management integration, especially beyond the dyadic level. There is also a lack of detailed frameworks and concrete recommendations for how supply chains can become more integrated (Naslund & Hulthen, 2012).

Despite the increasing interest in SCM by researchers and practitioners, there is still a lack of academic literature concerning topics such as methodologies to guide and support SCM evaluation. Most developed methodologies have been provided by consulting companies, are restricted in their publication, and use (Simon, Di Serio, Pires, & Martins, 2015).

Furthermore, the concept of SCM integration does not come without problems. Academic literature provides little, if any, empirical evidence of integration of supply chains beyond the dyadic level (Naslund & Hulthen, 2012).

Global Supply Chain Management and Technology

We are living in an uncertain world (Mamillo, 2015). Customers require more choices, better prices, high quality and better post-sale services; technology is changing quickly; suppliers are becoming less reliable. If organizations cannot satisfy customers, be at the leading edge of technology, and suppliers are not reliable, business leaders and organizations may lose competitive advantage (Mamillo, 2015).

Based on research in SCM innovation and trends, technology impacts global supply chain management (GSCM) at all levels of the supply chain: Born global firms. A new trend of organizations that forms alliances with suppliers relying heavily on trust and technology (Okoroafo, Gammoh, Koh, & Williams, 2015). Cost and quality are no longer efficient for traditional competition. Organization relying on technology for competitiveness (Albors-Garrigós, de Miguel-Molina, & de Miguel-Molina, 2014). Information communication technology (ICT) in relationship management (RM). (Gotore, Mutanga, & Mugwati, 2014).

Design and Methodology

Researchers have used various designs and methodologies to study innovation and trends, and especially technology in SCM. Researchers presented case studies, phenomenological studies, quantitative and qualitative approaches, and empirical studies. However, it remains that empirical studies are discovered by researchers to be more defined.

Research Findings

In the past researchers have focused on technology and how it affects global supply chain management (GSCM) with the use of RFID, ERP systems, supply chain technology (SCT), and the numerous and unmet expectations based on SCT (Saldanha, Mello, Knemeyer, & Vijayaraghavan, 2015). Single-use systems (SUS) in biopharmaceutical drug development and confidence in the technology has increased. With this shift has come a dependence on suppliers that is related to production capabilities, and this is a situation that did not previously exist (Challenger, 2014). Furthermore, ERP systems and learning about products from consumers is leading in technology with advantages (Odenwald & Berg, 2014).

With the increase in the use of technology, its misuse possibility also increases in general (Zhou & Piramuthu, 2013). Moreover, there are instances where new technologies are implemented without thoroughly testing for vulnerabilities. Researchers consider RFID, a disruptive technology, and related vulnerabilities in existing supply chain applications from an ethics perspective (Zhou & Piramuthu, 2013). They developed an extended ethics model to incorporate the effects of emerging information and communication technologies, specifically that of RFID systems, including technology selection, social consequences, and practitioners' rationality (Zhou & Piramuthu, 2013). Furthermore, they introduced a set of matrices for regulation technology development based on this model to serve as a communication tool for the policy maker for policy design regulation (Zhou & Piramuthu, 2013). Researchers use the case of RFID to illustrate the model and matrices (Zhou & Piramuthu, 2013).

The omnichannel environment presents new challenges and opportunities for both information and product fulfillment (Bell, Gallino, & Moreno, 2014). While all retailers need to effectively and efficiently manage fulfillment and information provision, there are important nuances to how this happens, depending on where and how the retailer got started and what kinds of improvement create the most leverage (Bell, Gallino, & Moreno, 2014). Researchers deliver a customer-focused framework showing how to win in the omnichannel environment through critical innovations in information delivery and product fulfillment (Bell, Gallino, & Moreno, 2014). The framework emerged from our research with both traditional and nontraditional retailers (Bell, Gallino, & Moreno, 2014). To thrive in the new environment, retailers of all stripes and origins need to deploy information and fulfillment strategies that reduce friction in every phase of the buying process (Bell, Gallino, & Moreno, 2014). This means simultaneously providing, in a cost-effective and narrative-enhancing way (Bell, Gallino, & Moreno, 2014).

Future Directions

The future is cloud computing value in SCM (Goel, 2015). However, a quick exchange of information and technology can be a challenge (Pivoda, 2014). Increase in technology can yield increase in misuse, and RFID, disruptive innovation, vulnerabilities (Zhou, & Piramuthu, 2013).

Moreover, retail customers are now "omnichannel" in their outlook and behavior — they use both online and offline retail channels readily and win in the omnichannel environment through critical innovations in information delivery and product fulfillment (Bell, Gallino, & Moreno, 2014).

Conclusion

In conclusion, Supply chains, supply chain management, and global supply chain management are terms used to create and manage products domestically and globally. There are various trends and innovations to supply chain management. Researchers reveal gaps in the literature and the need for continued research. Global supply chain management and technology is a trending aspect of supply chain management and leads to the enhancement of organization based on further research and studies. I presented in this study a background, analysis of the field and future contribution to supply chain management in terms of global supply chain management and technology.

Appendix A: An Example of a Global Supply Chain and Design

IASC-International Alliance for Strategic Change, Inc.

www.IASC.biz

IASC-International Alliance for Strategic Change, Inc. (IASC) is a start-up corporation; we have just completed our first line of service based on our product, the Innovative Solutions Strategy Plan (ISSP) for our client Friends of Street Kids and Orphans of Uganda (FOSKOF). IASCs strategy is to help multinational corporations (MNC) and other corporate enterprises expand their strategy into emerging and rural economies, and beginning with these markets in Sub-Sahara Africa (SSA). As Maria Ramos, Group Chief Executive of financial services company ABSA Group Ltd., South Africa, a division of the Barclays Group, comments of her global clients, the question that they get asked frequently is can they help their company does business in Africa, and the answer is straightforward and often times, not (Broadman, 2015). With IASC, the answer is straightforward, and always yes. However, to do this, an effective and efficient supply chain will need an implementation that provides optimal success for our company, and in turn, value for our stakeholders and customers.

The organization's supply chain is important in aligning with our strategy. Supply chain (SC) aligned with corporate strategy improves the firm's performance (Arora, 2014). IASC is an international consulting firm, and its supply chain is a reflection of human resources, technology, and intellectual property, as key components. The key stakeholders are all the suppliers and benefactors of the ISSP. They comprise of our full executive corporate suite (c-suite) board of directors, specialized consultants, field executives, corporate partners, the business education community, investors, potential stockholders, class B and C board members, outsourcing partners, strategically aligned collaborative partners, clients, and business communities. We depend on technologies such as the internet, social media, and mobile devices. Our vendors comprise of direct selling units that filter in through marketing on behalf of companies with products and services applicable to marketing in emerging economies, such as cosmetics and toiletries. Modes of transportation involved with IASC are those that we would use for traveling to clients such as airlines, and delivery of client presentations and products, such as Fed Ex.

The company's SC is in the implementation stages . Therefore, we will implement its design for maximizing effectiveness and harmony. The key inputs and outputs of IASCs supply chain IASC is a strategic alignment and collaboration of consulting firms and business owners doing business as a joint venture, therefore, the initial suppliers that merit partnership status are those of the collaboration. Other suppliers that merit partnership status are those that contribute to projects based on contracting consultant status with our company. We have a standard roster of consultants; however, we manage an exclusive consultant base with membership and board status. Their merited status is important because they provide value-added, working assistance and knowledge in fulfilling company projects.

IASC is an international consulting firm. Therefore, our SC design and strategy is global. We offer our partner base protection because our initial strategy and intent of the corporation is to maintain a cohesive and hyper-connective model. Our company has a motto of "One World One Place" and therefore our strategic considerations involve us relying on this facet.

Creating buy-in for my IASC SC design is an optimistic challenge. My board of advisors of the IASC c-suite is the first executives I will diligently seek for critical analysis and approval. However, my colleagues in this forum and the Walden community are essential to delivering analysis, advice, and justifications to enhance buy-in prior to an escalated proposal to board members. Input from stakeholders including clients is crucial to a competitive SC as well. One of the ways I will promote buy-in is to address the importance of supply chain management (SCM) and integration, especially for a global organization. Academic literature suggests that integration is a requirement and key characteristic for SC management and globalization is one reason for corporations to integrate their supply chain (Naslund & Hulthen, 2012). A working definition for SCM integration is the co-ordination and management of the upstream and downstream product, service, financial and, information flows of the core business processes between a focal company and its key suppliers and its key customers (Naslund & Hulthen, 2012). Focusing on this point, in terms of our global structure, I can enlighten stakeholders and viewers on extended perspectives outside the norms of SCM to consider along with the company's need to implement an original SC and design. This presentation eludes to the necessity of immediate SC buy-in and implementation as a precursor to future modification and design.

After initial executive buy-in, I would present my design to a group of key stakeholders such partnering consultants and field consultants by organizing a PowerPoint presentation that involved a demonstration of the new SC design, and an opportunity for key stakeholders to challenge and suggest potential redesigns. In my stance as a former educator, my approach would run as a facilitator of combined groups or team members. I would give the initial SC design along with chart paper and tools to each group so they may construct and enhancement or reconstructive new design of our SC. I would then allow each group to present their constructions or reconstruction while having an individual recorder notate suggestions for further consideration and implementation by the IASC board. Finally, I would videotape the presentation and discussion for future reference and review.

Chantell Beaty, IASC CEO, 2015

Appendix B: Annotated Bibliographies for Further Research

Okoroafo, S. C., Gammoh, B. S., Koh, A. C., & Williams, M. (2015). Global supply chain management strategies of born-global firms in the fashion industry: A conceptual model. *International Business Research, 8*, 97-105. doi:10.5539/ibr.v8n1p97

>The study examines the influence of trust, culture, and Web-enabled information technology on global supply chain management strategies of born global firms in the fashion industry. The paper seeks to provide insights into the success (or otherwise) of such entrepreneurial firms as they manage their business network alliances in the design, production, delivery and marketing of a fashion product...a product that is characterized by a very short fad/fashion product lifecycle. The authors develop a conceptual model that links partnership formation, contracting processes, and global supply chain management strategies to the firm's performance. Future research efforts need to empirically investigate the conceptual model on a sample of born global firms in the fashion industry.

Albors-Garrigós, J., de Miguel-Molina, B., & de Miguel-Molina, M. (2014). The role of the global value chain in new competitive environments: The case of mature industries. *IBIMA Business Review, 2014*, 1-17. doi: 10.5171/2014.210236

>As a result of the growth of emergent economies and globalization, the traditional industry models based on competition relying on costs and quality are not sufficient for traditional industry competitiveness. These classical paradigms considered that clustered industries based their competitiveness on technology innovation and the use of cluster

internal and external resources. However, from the point of view of global value chains, knowledge management combined with an adequate relationship marketing strategy brings an innovative way of considering the sustainability of clustered firms. The objective of this article is presenting a research which will analyze the governance structure of the value chain in the territorial of tile ceramic Spanish cluster, and the past and present roles of the most relevant stakeholders in the value creation system. The research methodology will follow both quantitative and qualitative approaches. The paper will conclude that there is a paradigm change where traditional chain agents are losing their control and leadership in their contribution to the creation of value, and new agents appear with a more stable and relevant contribution and role.

Saldanha, J. P., Mello, J. E., Knemeyer, A. M., & Vijayaraghavan, T. A. S. (2015).

    Implementing supply chain technologies in emerging markets: and institutional theory. *Journal of Supply Chain Management, 51*, 5-26. doi: 10.1111/jscm.12065

    Supply chain technology (SCT) facilitates information transfer within and across firm boundaries. However, institutional environments in emerging markets give rise to challenges that inhibit the implementation of SCT and the consequent realization of its benefits. Unfortunately, there is a lack of understanding as to the nature or the extent of these implementation challenges. We undertook a grounded theory study in the emerging market of India to investigate how SCT is implemented when subjected to prevailing institutional pressures. Based on an analysis of interviews with 50 supply chain managers, we find that early adopters of SCT experience significant and numerous unmet expectations associated with SCT implementation. These unmet expectations arise from competing for institutional logics with the resultant isomorphic pressure causing the juxtaposition of two incompatible supply chains in India. A key finding of this study contradicts extant research, supporting recent work in emerging markets, to suggest a need to reassess our mental models developed in the West and conceptualize de novo models that are sensitive to the institutional environments of emerging markets.

Challener, C. A., (2014). Securing the single-use supply chain. *Pharmaceutical Technology Europe, 26*, 24-28. Retrieved from http://www.scimagojr.com/journalsearch.php?q=21127&tip=sid

> Ross Acucena]. "The need is security of supply," agrees Kevin Ott, executive director of the BioProcess Systems Alliance (bpsa). He adds that dual sourcing is one possible solution, but there are others with fewer validation challenges, including redundant supply sources from a single vendor and inventory plans, for example. "The question," he continues, "also becomes complicated by how far back in the supply chain one needs to go.

Goel, R. (2015). Trusted supply chains: Surveying competitive value of the cloud. *International Journal of Management & Information Systems (Online), 19*(1), 43-n/a. Retrieved from

> Cloud computing has become a force multiplier for organizations as they realize the benefit from the shared computing platforms and services offered by cloud computing. Providers market shared computing platforms and services because of their convenience, dynamism, elasticity, and scalability to meet the growing demands of

organizations, specifically in widespread supply chain networks. Yet, the issuance of trust has become a concern in the cloud web as cloud computing service technologies advance faster than measures to secure it. This research presents a framework to determine which specific supply chain functions can derive the most value from cloud capabilities and to understand how to leverage these technologies strategically to develop a competitive advantage. It proposes a strategic integration of cloud functionalities to create profitable supply chain network partnerships and to improve the processes, quality and innovation potential in the overall Supply Chain Management (SCM), while maintaining a trusted cloud environment.

Gotore, I., Mutanga, M., & Mugwati, M. (2014). Towards growth and profitability through relationship marketing: The case of the Tyre Manufacturing Industry in Zimbabawe. *International Journal of Marketing and Technology, 4*, 1-15. Retrieved from http://www.inderscience.com/jhome.php?jcode=ijtmkt

The study sought to explore the role of customer relationship management in generating growth and sustaining profitability in the tyre manufacturing industry of Zimbabwe. The main objectives were to find out the level of awareness of the relationship marketing concept within tyre manufacturing companies in Zimbabwe; to evaluate the level of adoption and implementation of relationship marketing by players within the tyre manufacturing industry and to find out the contribution to profitability and business growth of relationship marketing in the tyre manufacturing industry. The study recommends that tyre manufacturing companies broaden their view of customer relations and incorporate the use of information communication technology to help implement lifetime relationships with their clients and stimulate corporate growth. The study also recommends that the organisations undergo a culture reform and align all their employees in all departments, to the demands and needs of ideal and effective relationship.

Odenwald, T., & Berg, C. (2014). A new perspective on enterprise resource management. *MIT Sloan Management Review, 56*, 12-14. Retrieved from http://sloanreview.mit.edu/

Being able to answer questions about the safety and environmental effects of products we use is critical. However, without the right information, even seemingly easy questions are difficult to answer. We send space crafts to Mars, but we know embarrassingly little about everyday products we use. Although we produce huge quantities of data every second, we frequently lack the relevant and actionable data points to respond to simple questions people have about what products are made of and how they are made. For the most part, today's information systems and reporting methods treat factors such as emissions, waste and employee protections as externalities. But many factors, including economic uncertainty, population growth, climate change and escalating demand for natural resources, are placing new pressures on companies to take a broader set of considerations into account when making decisions.

Pivoda, R. (2014). Challenges and risks to manage sustainability throughout the value. *Economics, Management and Financial Markets, 9*, 296-302. Retrieved from http://www.addletonacademicpublishers.com/economics-management-and-financial-markets

Today's world of business is even more significantly shaped by the trend of globalization while the expected life of a company got much shorter. The cutthroat competition in saturated markets, the growing scarcity of the resources, the quick exchange of information and the new technologies available worldwide mean that daily, a company has to face a lot of challenges in order to survive. Moreover, the customers put pressure on companies by expecting from them cheap but high quality products that are environment-friendly. This means that sustainability management in a company is no more a matter of choice, but an absolute must in order to keep the competitive advantage.

Zhou, W., & Piramuthu, S. (2013). Technology regulation policy for business ethics: An example of RFID in supply chain   management. *Journal of Business Ethics, 116*, 327-340. doi:10.1007/s10551-012-1474-4

With the increase in use of a technology, its misuse possibility also increases in general. Moreover, there are instances where new technologies are implemented without thoroughly testing for vulnerabilities. We consider RFID, a disruptive technology, and related vulnerabilities in existing supply chain applications from an ethics perspective. We develop an extended ethics model to incorporate the effects of emerging information and communication technologies, specifically that of RFID systems, including technology selection, social consequences, and practitioners' rationality. We introduce a set of matrices for technology regulation development based on this model to serve as a communication tool for the policy maker for policy design regulation. We use the case of RFID to illustrate the model and matrices.

Bell, D. R., Gallino, S., & Moreno, A. (2014). How to win in an omnichannel world. *MIT Sloan Management Review, 56*, 45-53. Retrieved from http://sloanreview.mit.edu/

The omnichannel environment presents new challenges and opportunities for both information and product fulfillment. While all retailers need to effectively and efficiently manage fulfillment and information provision, there are important nuances to how this happens, depending on where and how the retailer got started and what kinds of improvement create the most leverage. This article delivers a customer-focused framework showing how to win in the omni-channel environment through critical innovations in information delivery and product fulfillment. The framework emerged from our research with both traditional and nontraditional retailers. To thrive in the new environment, retailers of all stripes and origins need to deploy information and fulfillment strategies that reduce friction in every phase of the buying process. This means simultaneously providing, in a cost-effective and narrative-enhancing way,

References

Arora, A. (2014). Sustainability Strategies in Supply Chain Management. Electronic Theses & Dissertations. Retrieved from http://digitalcommons.georgiasouthern.edu/etd/1063

Azadegan, A., Dooley, K. J., Carter, P. L., & Carter, J. R. (2008). Supplier innovativeness and the role of inter organizational learning in enhancing manufacturer. *Journal of Supply Chain Management*, 44, 14-35. Retrieved from http://onlinelibrary.wiley.com/journal/10.1111/%28ISSN%291745-493X

Boyson, S., Corsi, T., Dresner, M., & Harrington, L. (2007). World trade reader research: Global supply chain management style depends on company size and scale. World Trade, 20, 32-34, 36. Retrieved from http://connection.ebscohost.com/c/articles/27072812/world-trade-reader-research-global-supply-chain-management-style-depends-company-size-scale

Broadman, H.G. (2015). Competing for African markets: Strategies to win new business now. Retrieved from http://www.pwc.com/us/en/view/issue-16/strategies-win-african-business.jhtml

Cassivi, L., Hadaya, P., Lefebvre, E., & Lefebvre, L. A. (2008). The role of collaboration on process, relational, and product innovations in a supply chain. *International Journal of E-Collaboration*, 4, 11-32. Retrieved from http://www.igi-global.com/journal/international-journal-collaboration-ijec/1090

Greer, B. M., & Theuri, P. (2012). Linking supply chain management superiority to multifaceted firm financial performance. Journal of Supply Chain Management, 48(3), 97-106. Retrieved from http://search.proquest.com/docview/1467435425?accountid=14872

Näslund, D., & Hulthen, H. (2012). Supply chain management integration: a critical

analysis. Benchmarking, 19, 481–501. doi:10.1108/14635771211257963

Handfield, R. B., & Lawson, B. (2007). Integrating suppliers into new product

development. Research Technology Management, 50, 44-51. Retrieved from

http://www.iriweb.org:8080/Main/Library/RTM_Journal/Public_Site/Navigation/

Publications/Research-Technology_Management/index.aspx?hkey=a684bca1-0bed-

4520-83eb-b8e4df9c6b9b

Malik, Y., and Ruwadi, B. (2011). Building the supply chain of the future. Retrived from

http://www.mckinsey.com/insights/operations/building_the_supply_chain_of_the_future

PR Newswire (2014, Jul 22). Global supply chain management (SCM) software market 2014-

2018. Retrieved from http://www.prnewswire.com/

Parker, D. B., Zsidisin, G. A., & Ragatz, G. L. (2008). Timing and the extent of supplier

integration in new product development: A contingency approach. Supply Chain

Management, 44, 71-83. Retrieved from

http://onlinelibrary.wiley.com/journal/10.1111/%28ISSN%291745-493X

Soosay, C. A., Hyland, P.W., & Ferrer, M. (2008). Supply chain collaboration: Capabilities for

continuous innovation. Supply Chain Management, 13, 160-169. Retrieved from the

http://onlinelibrary.wiley.com/journal/10.1111/%28ISSN%291745-493X

Wisner, J. D., & Keah, C. T. (2000). Supply chain management and its impact on

purchasing. Supply Chain Management, 36, 33-42. Retrieved from

http://onlinelibrary.wiley.com/journal/10.1111/%28ISSN%291745-493X

Alexander, G., & Bonaparte, N. (2008). My way or the highway that I built. Ancient Dictators, 25(7), 14-31. doi:10.8220/CTCE.52.1.23-91

Babar, E. (2007). The art of being a French elephant. Adventurous Cartoon Animals, 19, 4319-4392. Retrieved from http://www.elephants104.ace.org

Bumstead, D. (2009). The essentials: Sandwiches and sleep. Journals of Famous Loafers, 5, 565-582. doi:12.2847/CEDG.39.2.51-71

Hansel, G., & Gretel, D. (1973). Candied houses and unfriendly occupants. Thousand Oaks, CA: Fairy Tale Publishing.

Hera, J. (2008). Why Paris was wrong. Journal of Greek Goddess Sore Spots, 20(4), 19-21.

Investopedia (2015). Supply Chain Definition. Retrieved from http://www.investopedia.com/terms/s/supplychain.asp

Laureate, Education, Inc. (Producer). (2007). How to cite a video: The city is always Baltimore [DVD]. Baltimore, MD: Author.

Mamillo, D. (2015). Supply chain collaboration under uncertainty in the albanian beer market. Management Dynamics in the Knowledge Economy, 3(1), 99-117. Retrieved from http://search.proquest.com/docview/1674357185?accountid=14872

Simon, A. T., Di Serio, L. C., Pires, S. R. I., & Martins, G. S. (2015). Evaluating supply chain management: A methodology based on a theoretical model. Revista De Administração Contemporânea, 19(1), 26-44. Retrieved from http://search.proquest.com/docview/1652867030?accountid=14872

Sinatra, F. (2008). Zing! Went the strings of my heart. Making Good Songs Great, 18(3), 31-32. Retrieved from http:///articlesextollingrecordingsofyore.192/fs.com

Smasfaldi, H., Wareumph, I., Aeoli, Q., Rickies, F., Furoush, P., Aaegrade, V., ... Fiiel, B. (2005). The art of correcting surname mispronunciation. New York, NY: Supportive Publisher Press. Retrieved from http://www.onewaytociteelectronicbooksperAPA7.02.com

White, S., & Red, R. (2001). Stop and smell the what now? Floral arranging for beginners (Research Report No. 40-921). Retrieved from University of Wooded Glen, Center for Aesthetic Improvements in Fairy Tales website: http://www.uwg.caift/~40_921

Okoroafo, S. C., Gammoh, B. S., Koh, A. C., & Williams, M. (2015). Global supply chain management strategies of born-global firms in the fashion industry: A conceptual model. International Business Research, 8, 97-105. doi:10.5539/ibr.v8n1p97

www.ingramcontent.com/pod-product-compliance
Lightning Source LLC
Chambersburg PA
CBHW070303190526
45169CB00004B/1512